Compass Life

My Journey
Through
Breast Cancer

Authored By
Debra Rouse

PATASKITY PUBLISHING CO.

Pataskity Publishing Co.
207 Hudson Terrance Suite 102
Augusta, GA 30906
pataskitypublishing.com
(706) 250-3956

Thank you...

Thank you to my loving husband, Dr. Deshawn Rouse.

Thank you to my wonderful sons: Tarique, Kenly, Jordan and my bonus son, Jeremiah.

Thank you to my loving family especially to my mother, Janice and my sister, Shaunya. You all have never ceased to amaze me by your support, showing up, and love.

Thank you to my supportive church family.

Dedication

My husband has been telling me for years that I should write a book. I dedicate this book to him for the vision that he saw over my life, and for him speaking this book into existence.

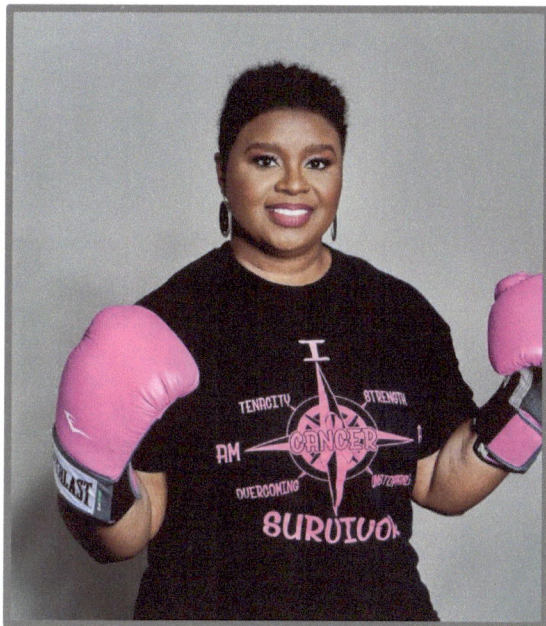

About The Author

Debra Rouse is a wife, mother, first lady, minister and a published author. She was born and raised in the small town of Andrews, South Carolina where everyone seems to know each other. Her husband knew she was going to be his wife long before the two were married, and he pursued her until she became Mrs. Debra Rouse. Currently, the two have been married for twenty-one plus years, and are blessed to have a beautiful family, built a thriving church and created a lifetime of memories.

Table Of Contents

Abstract
What Is A Compass?
My Divine Direction

I t is just like the monotheistic God to connect all things: old, new, wise and or foolish together to result in our good. After all, the Bible teaches us in 1st Corinthians 1:27A, *"But God hath chosen the foolish things of the world to confound the wise;"* this statement exemplifies that my experiences have all been to use as a compass for me, and even to bless someone else. According to Wikipedia, a compass is *"a device that shows the cardinal directions used for navigation and geographical orientation. It commonly consists of a magnetized needle or other elements such as a compass card or compass rose, which can pivot to align itself with magnetic North."* In layman's terms, a compass gives you direction to the place, or area you would like to go.

I experienced what I call a *"spiritual compass."* This helped me to navigate through the journey of having cancer. Through my faith, my belief and trust in God, I was able to take God at His word and believe that He was going to bring me out of this! During my journey, I traveled some treacherous terrain at times, and I did not think I had the strength to pull through but I made it! God spoke through His Word in Psalms 119:105, *"Thy word is a lamp unto my feet and a light unto my path."* God showed me the way, and I can assure you that He would do the same for you! Just ask Him and let Him lead.

I recall that it was vacation time, vacation time, vacation time! We were on the road again back to Asheville, North Carolina to the Biltmore Mansion. My husband decided that we would skip our regular summer scheduled vacation, and do something different for Thanksgiving. We set out early Wednesday morning to Asheville. The ride was pretty fair and the weather was cool. Once we got there, we stopped to have lunch. After lunch, we went to our hotel rooms to rest. Our rooms were so nice and comfortable. We stood on the balcony, and saw different shops, eateries, a theater and the YMCA. Everything was within walking distance from the hotel! This place reminded me of the Market Commons in Myrtle Beach, South Carolina.

The visit to the Biltmore Mansion was simply amazing! We countered through the entire mansion, absorbing the breathtaking Christmas trees and decorations that were in every room. In the mansion, each room is dressed with a Christmas tree during this time of the year. I do not think I have the patience to dress my own house with a Christmas tree in every room! After sightseeing through the house, we visited the little shops on the other side of the property buying sweet treats and hot cocoa. We stopped to take a few photos under the lights, and headed back to the hotel to call it a day.

Waking up to a frosty Thanksgiving morning, we opted out of breakfast. We relaxed and hung out before making our trek to Hendersonville, North Carolina to the Golden Corral restaurant. This will be the first time we would have eaten at a restaurant for Thanksgiving dinner. This was something new for us! Upon our arrival, there was a line already formed on the outside of the restaurant. We were in shock to see the amount of people waiting to enter. We hopped in line like the rest of the patrons, and braved the chilly winds until we made it into the restaurant. Warm never felt so good once we got inside! The hustle and bustle of hungry patrons, staff, waiters and waitresses was a little chaotic, but we managed to find a table and got settled. My boys were ready to eat and so was I. We ate and laughed, and ate and laughed again! After a few trips to the hot bars, we noticed another family joined our little section of the restaurant.

They were enjoying their meal, like the rest of us, especially the baby. There she was a blonde-haired baby girl sitting in a high chair enjoying her first Thanksgiving meal being fed by who we assumed to be her mom. Nostalgia kicked in while I looked at the baby and her mother. I cannot remember the times I fed my sons while they sat in a highchair and repeatedly kicked my leg over and over. After a while, my husband and I noticed that the baby was not making any noise. We turned in their direction, and saw the mom holding the baby's arm up in the air saying the baby is not breathing. The baby looked lifeless.

By that time, the young waitress rushed over. The grandmother picked up the baby, and began hitting her back as if she was choking. I yelled to them twice, *"Turn her upside down and slap her back!"* They did not comply. I jumped up from my family where I was sitting, briskly walked over to them, snatched the baby from the grandmother, and began the *Heimlich Maneuver* on the baby. While all of this was going on, the mother of the baby was praying, and trying to help me, but she was getting in my way. After a few slaps on the back, I heard the waitress say,

"Let's see if she is breathing." During this excruciating tense moment, my husband told me that the people in our section were crying and praying looking onward as this chaotic event unfolded. I lifted the baby upward, and I felt her chest go in and out. I asked for a napkin to clean her nose which had food coming out of it. Then the baby cried and I handed her back to her mom; I knew then that she was alright. As I walked to my seat, everyone in the section had a look of relief on their faces. I fixed my clothes and sat down with my family. Families started clapping and saying, *"thank you"* to me and I was like, *"no problem, glad I could do it."* We finished our Thanksgiving dinner with huge smiles on our faces. Before leaving, we went by the baby's table to check on her and the family. The mom took a picture of the baby and me and thanked me again. We exchanged names and took more pictures. We said our goodbyes, hopped into the car and proceeded to the hotel. My boys were impressed, and so excited about what I did for the baby. I had a proud mommy moment because I would want someone to do that for my boys if they were in distress.

After settling in for the night, we were watching television and saw the family from Golden Corral. They contacted the news station to thank me, and find out more about me. *We were stunned!* The mom, Hannah even looked me up on Facebook and found me. My photo with the baby was plastered all over the television. *I was in total shock!* Hannah and I talked and met each other with the baby. She came to the hotel with flowers for me. Also, a reporter came and interviewed us. It was awesome seeing them again! I had numerous interviews from television stations and from all over. I did an interview over the radio; I did a podcast as well. I saw my picture on the national news, Fox. I could not believe it. People were congratulating me, and they made me feel like a celebrity! I just thanked God for being in the right place at the right time. With the new found fame, my hometown even named December 15th as Debra Rouse Day. I wondered to myself, *"Who would have thought?"* One simple act of kindness turned into these beautiful gestures towards me. I did not perform the *Heimlich maneuver* on the baby for recognition; I did it to save the baby's life! God used me to be a compass to save a baby's life and I am forever grateful. I thank Him for my divine direction. We must always remember that we are purposeful, and designed to help, teach and bless those whom God allows to cross our paths. If we are following the compass He has for us, we will do this both consciously and unconsciously.

What Is This! My Divine Lump

Two thousand nineteen rolled in, and I was thankful to God for another year! Time flies! A New Year, new exciting things and birthdays. Yes, I said, "Birthdays!" The Lord decided to bless my husband and I with three handsome sons, each of whom are born in the month of January. Can you believe it? And to top it off my husband and I have our wedding anniversary during the month of January. The celebration did not stop this month and I loved every moment of it. All three boys as they got older wanted to celebrate their birthdays separately. They were coming into their own personalities and wanted to do their own thing. My husband and I allowed our sons to pick the restaurant they wanted to go to and we would take them there for their birthday. We love to celebrate birthdays in our household. For our anniversary, my husband and I usually go away for the weekend, or we'll go out to dinner. It is nothing like spending time with the one you're in love with!

By the end of January, my family and I would have celebrated all of our birthdays, anniversaries and now it was time for us to return back to a normal life. At least this is what I thought! I was taking a shower, and I did a self-breast examination. I felt a small lump in my right breast. Of course, I was concerned, but I did not want to become frantic. I knew I had an upcoming appointment with my gynecologist, and I planned to make her aware of my experiences at that time. I did not tell my husband as of yet. I kept watching the lump for any changes in size and feeling. By the end of February, I noticed discharge from my nipple. I knew this was not right and my concern heightened. Still, I did not make my husband aware of these changes because I wanted to get it checked first.

Once the month of March arrived, I was excited because my birthday is on March 7th. The last few birthdays before this one were filled with sorrow. My father died on March 3, 2016 (*four days before my 40th birthday*). I was thinking about celebrating my 40th birthday; however, that came to a screeching halt, and every birthday after that has been a bit sorrowful. This year, I wanted to do something or go somewhere different. With that being said, my baby sister, Shaunya told me that she had a surprise for me. I was excited because I like surprises around my birthday! I could not wait to find out what the surprise that she had in store for me was. I was like a kid in a candy store! While my excitement was on one-hundred, I still had to deal with this lump. Eventually, I went to my doctor's appointment, and I explained to her my findings during my self- examination. My doctor scheduled an appointment which consisted of two different tests. I felt good because I figured we were on the right track.

In the meantime my sister told me some bad news. My birthday trip was canceled! My heart sunk as I was thinking to myself, "*This is another birthday setback.*" She explained that our plane, the Boeing 737 Max, was grounded due to two plane crashes killing everyone on board. She also sent me our itinerary for where we were going. She was taking me to Los Angeles, California! I was totally devastated. While she tried her best to get another flight, she could not. We realized that it was not meant for us to go. That made my day miserable!

Because I had already put in to have days off, I just kept it that way. The night before my sister and I were supposed to leave, my husband said to me, "*I am going to miss you.*" I proceeded to tell him my birthday disappointment. The next morning, my sister brought us breakfast. She was disappointed and mad just like I was because she knew what I've gone through the last few birthdays. After I got dressed, I was sitting on the bed thinking about riding out by myself. My husband rushed into our bedroom, grabbed me, and hugged me real tight. He said through tears, *"I am glad that you are here. I had a dream you were on a plane and it went down."* My husband had this dream before learning that the plane fell to the ground. I held him tight and began to cry!

As the month went on, our family was hit hard with the passing of my uncle. My Uncle James had pancreatic cancer and he lost the battle on March 20, 2019. This is the first child out of ten that have died. God knows when you need a *"pick me up!"* Out of the sorrows of this month, came some rays of sunshine. The contractor broke ground for the building of our new home. I came home one day from work, and saw the contractors in my yard. I screamed like a kid, and ran in the house! My husband stood by our dinner table with a bouquet of red roses. Jazz music filled the house, and I literally jumped into his arms. We danced to the song, *"Don't Worry About A Thing."* That was a very beautiful moment. He promised to build me a house, and it was getting built in my front yard.

Growing In Faith Through Changes
Mammogram

My appointment for my mammogram was scheduled for April 10, 2019. I went with an open mind as I believed God for a great outcome! I had a mammogram and then an ultrasound. Following, I was told by the sonographer that something was in one of my milk ducts, but that I should not be alarmed. She explained that she had seen this a lot and it may not be anything to worry about. I took her advice into consideration; however, I still had a lump in my breast that had not gone away. In the meantime, while waiting on my mammogram results, my family and I went to Florida to see my aunt and cousins. We stayed the weekend in

Jacksonville, Florida. I had a great time. My mom was dying to get to the zoo, so we took her. The weather was pretty and we enjoyed ourselves to the fullest; so much, we forgot to go by the beach! My second oldest wanted to put his feet in the Florida waters. I guess we would have to make another trip.

Once I returned home, I received my mammogram results. I was glad that the mammogram did not show any abnormalities in my breast, but I still had a lump and there was discharge from my right breast. The matter did not sit too well with my gynecologist either, so she sent me to a breast surgeon. On April 30th, I walked into the breast surgeon's office. While I did not see the doctor, I saw the Physician Assistant (PA). She was very nice and attentive to my needs and questions. She checked my breast, felt the lump, and also took some of the discharge to test it. She shared with me that blood was in the discharge, and that was not a good sign. The PA immediately scheduled me an appointment for a second mammogram, and for the first time, I was scheduled to have a biopsy.

I called my job and told them that I was not coming in due to another test! I waited in my car for my next appointment, as I wondered, "*What is going to become of these tests? What answer will I get from these tests?*" I got to my appointment, and to my disappointment, the doctor said it was not an area that she saw on the mammogram to do the biopsy. I was shocked because the PA was certain something was going on, and now this doctor is saying something totally different. I left the office feeling bewildered. I did not know what to think. All I knew was that I have this lump and discharge was coming from my breast, and this is not normal. The PA called to set up another appointment for an MRI, and this time a double biopsy on each breast.

I left the office with all kinds of thoughts going through my mind. I knew something was not right. The PA knew something was not right, but now we have to wait again for another test. I was trying to stay positive by thinking good thoughts, but seeing the discharge and feeling the lump began to make it very hard to walk by faith and not by sight. I knew God was in control, but I questioned the trial that He was allowing in my life.

Learning My Diagnosis
My Initial Shock

Tuesday May 14, 2019 started off like any other workday. I got up at my regular time and got ready. While driving to Georgetown, I prepared my mind for another workday and patients. I also reflected on what was ahead of me in the next few hours. Despite what I was experiencing, I tried to keep focus and remain calm. I left work at 11:00 AM to tackle the terrible traffic in Charleston. *Oh, I detest the traffic in Charleston!* It is bumper-to-bumper all day every day. It is fast driving like the Daytona Speedway. I arrived at Roper Medical Hospital and to the office where I was being seen. I checked in and they called me back a few minutes later. A technician walked me back to the changing room where I got undressed from the waist up. I removed all of my jewelry. I slipped on a gown and waited for the tech to come get me.

Once it was my turn to be seen, I followed her into the room where it was cold. I saw a big MRI machine, and was thinking, *"I have never experienced going in this type of machine before."* Not knowing what to expect, I remained calm and prayed. The technician placed an intravenous (IV) medication in my hand, and told me that I would be lying face down in the machine. After helping me up onto the table, she situated my breasts into two separate sides. They squeezed both breasts in the contraption which felt like cinder blocks were crushing my little breasts. I could not move at all! My head was on a soft pillow, and I was looking down. My arms were outstretched above my head. Needless to say, I was not comfortable. The tech left the room and began the test. My body was sliding back into the MRI to take the images of my breasts. After about ten minutes, the tech slid me out and administered the medical dye through the IV. Once I got back into the MRI, more pictures of my breasts were taken.

After the test was over Dr. H came into the room. She started giving me a topical anesthesia on the right breast first. She was explaining the biopsy procedure as she gave me the anesthesia. She then took a medical device which sounded like a drill, cut a slit into my breast, and began taking samples of breast tissue. I was almost in tears because of the discomfort and the thought of what was going on. Dr. H began to tell me that she was placing two small metal clips in my breast where she took the biopsy. She proceeded to do the same procedure on the left breast. All I could do was lay there in pain. Once Dr. H was done, I carefully crawled off of the table. The technician helped me down because my arms were sore from being stretched out over my head. I got dressed and the technician walked me over to another part of the hospital. There, another technician performed a mammogram on both breasts. All the pressure on my already painful breasts!! I could not believe this woman could be this cruel, but I know she was doing her job.

After being pulled and prodded, I was glad when I reached my car in the parking garage. My breasts were swollen and painful. The technician gave me small ice packs to place on them. I wish I had brought someone to drive home because I was not feeling like it! I arrived home, still in pain and ready to just lay down. I told my husband about my experience and how unpleasant it was. I could not hug my kids because my chest was still hurting. I was just ready for this day to be over along with the pain!

On Wednesday, May 15, 2019, a new day renewed mercies God extended my way. God also extended strength to me that I did not know I needed. My day was routine as usual, up and ready for work, and out the door. I was working in the business office. I worked in an optical shop twice a week and the business office three times a week. The day went as usual with lots of paperwork, filing, and getting invoices ready for the CFO. After I had my usual late lunch, I returned back to my desk. Today, I was scheduled to get off at 4:30 PM. I was excited that it was not 5:00 PM; thirty minutes earlier sounded terrific.

A little after 3:00 PM, a call came through for me. I got up to go to the back for more privacy. I went into one of the doctors' offices. I began speaking with the Physician's Assistant for my initial appointment that got this ball rolling. Her first words were, *"I did not want to call you at work, but I knew you wanted the results."* I said to her, *"Yes, mam."* She began talking to me about my left breast first. She said everything was good. The Physician's Assistant proceeded to talk to me about the right breast. She said my results showed Non-Invasive Ductal Carcinoma in Situ and Invasive Ductal Carcinoma in my right breast. I heard her loud and clear when she said, *"It is cancer."* While she was informing me of this intruder in my body, I grabbed a sticky note and began writing all of this down. Tears fell down my cheeks. I could not believe this was happening to me!

Some of what she said got drowned out in my *thoughts* that were going off in my head. I finished my conversation with the PA, and wiped my face as I left the doctor's office hoping not to run into anyone. I quickly walked to the bathroom. Once I was in there, I just fell to pieces. I placed my hands over my mouth, and I began to cry as my face drenched with tears. I was in shock at what was happening to me! I stayed in the bathroom for a few minutes just crying. I had cancer.

Knowing I had to get back to my desk, I thought to myself, "*I have got to get myself together.*" I blew my nose and wiped off my face. I walked back to my desk and looked at my phone. The time showed 3:34 PM. That time is now forever branded in my brain like a tattoo. Who goes back to work after getting a cancer diagnosis??!! I do! I started back working like nothing ever happened. I said to myself, "*You only got one hour left!*" I kept myself composed for the duration of that hour. I clocked out at 4:30 PM, got into my car and the water works came! The ride home was nothing short of a mini tsunami of tears. Questions were popping in my head and out of my mouth, "*Why is this happening to me? Why me? What did I do to deserve this?*" Questions, questions, questions. "*How do I process this?*" The twenty to twenty-five minute ride home was long and horrible. I was ready to get home, and I wanted the day to end. I pulled into the driveway, and got out of the car. While I wiped my face, I knew the dam was about to break again. I walked into my bedroom; my husband was ironing. Immediately, I threw my purse and jacket on the bed and just rushed to him. I put my arms around him as he was ironing. He placed his arms around me and I whispered, *"I have breast cancer."* The room grew still, sad and quiet. It was like the whole house heard what I said and suddenly became quiet too.

It was like time stood still for just a moment. Oh, I bawled my eyes out! My husband held me and allowed me to rest on his chest. I cried until I could not cry anymore. I removed myself from his grip, and immediately demanded my husband not to tell anyone! I told him, *"Do not say anything to my mom, kids or my church family yet because I am still processing what is happening. I am hurt, angry and devastated."* I wanted to know why God allowed this to happen to me. *Haven't I been a good Christian?* In my mind, I reflected on how there have been times when God used my hands and mouth for healing others. Now, this is happening to me. Needless to say, the night was long and restless. I could not help but to think that this disease is growing inside of my body, and I cannot do anything about it. This is the first *real* situation that I could not fix! This matter is big unlike if it was one of my boys' bruises that I could clean and patch! I could not bandage this up; I was not able to fix this, and to accept that I could not fix this situation was the most challenging part of my diagnosis.

This Is Not A Dream And It Begins

Another morning has come and I am still in disbelief! Truly, I was wishing that today would prove that I was dreaming about what just happened to me; however, I was definitely wrong. The total shock had consumed me, and I was not feeling work today. I should have stayed home but I did not. While at work, I just kept to myself. I did not feel like socializing with anyone, not even the patients. I felt like a zombie walking around aimlessly. For lunch, I sat in my car. No food, nothing to drink, just me and my thoughts. And my thoughts were winning! To my surprise my husband pulled up in front of me. I saw another person in the car; it was my mom. I am trying now to figure out why my husband and my mom are here at my job. I was wondering, "*Why isn't my mom at work?*" My husband came to the passenger side window, and placed his hand nervously on the door. He opened his mouth. I could not believe what was coming out of it. He said, *"Debra, I told your mom that you had cancer."* I thought to myself, *"If looks could definitely kill, he would be dead right now."* He said, *"I figured that because she's a woman she could relate to you better."* I seethed through clenched teeth and said, *"I told you not to tell anyone!"* I wanted to tell my mom when I had more information, but that was canceled.

My mom walked over to the driver side of my car. Her first question was, *"D, how are you doing?"*

I thought to myself, *"And it begins..."* I knew the questions were going to start, and I was not prepared neither feeling like this today. That is why I told my husband not to tell anyone! I told my mom I was not feeling too good about my diagnosis. I was not ready to tell her yet because I needed to process this whole situation. Next, came questions about who and when am I going to tell the family. I had to stress to her that I am not saying anything to anyone, and I do not want her to tell anyone. Lunch was over, just like that. Thirty minutes goes by fast, and this time I was thankful that time was on my side. I did not want to talk anymore. That whole situation was exhausting! Whenever processing a circumstance so painful, silence can be the best comfort. To say out loud,

"I have cancer" was one of the most painful things I could do. It made me cry. It hurt, so yes, I was lost for words and searching for my response to what life had thrown at me. While I returned back to work, my mind was somewhere else.

The days went on and I aimed to keep life as normal as possible. I cried in my car. My bathroom became my sanctuary as I cried there alone. I was trying to formulate in my mind how I was going to tell our boys. I did not want to sound defeated or down and out to them. I needed to be strong for them. Although I was the one experiencing grief, pain and every bit of what seemed abnormal circumstances, my heart desired to be strong for my sons.

Sunday, May 19, 2019 was not just an ordinary Sunday. It was the day I was going to be brave enough to tell our boys that I have cancer. *How do you really prepare for this?* We went to church as usual, no changes there. Our church services are always good but I couldn't help but think of my diagnosis. I was already letting this disease consume me. I was allowing it to get to me, and my faith was shaken a little. I did not understand what was going on! After Sunday dinner, my family and I sat in the den. I remember my oldest son, Tarique, was doing some writing and the rest of them were watching TV. I walked into the den and sat beside my husband. I told the boys I had something to tell them. I did not make a long speech; I just came out and told them about my doctor's visit and that I did not know exactly all the details about my diagnosis. But I had cancer.

There truly was a stillness in the air, everything was quiet, again. I asked each of them how they felt about the situation. Our youngest son, Jordan, said to me, *"I just don't want you to lose your hair."* Our middle son, Kenly said to me, *"I am very sad about this."* My oldest son dropped his head. I said to him, *"You are the oldest. Do you have anything to say?"* He looked at me and said, *"I hate that you have to go through this mom."* If anyone knows me, my boys mean more than the world to me. I felt like I was breaking their hearts. That was really tough. My husband ended the conversation by giving the family encouraging words of hope to know that we are believing in God, and He is still a healer. I never thought in a million years that I would be having a conversation with my boys about cancer.

A Picture Is Worth A Thousand Words

My Photo Journey

What a blessing during a very trying time!
I called my new house, my saving grace.

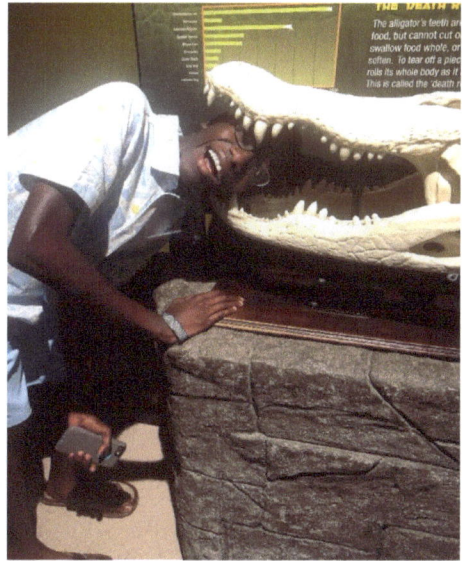

*Pics from our trip to the Ohio Aquarium.
The facial expressions tell it all.*

Lost all my hair, this is what chemotherapy does to you.

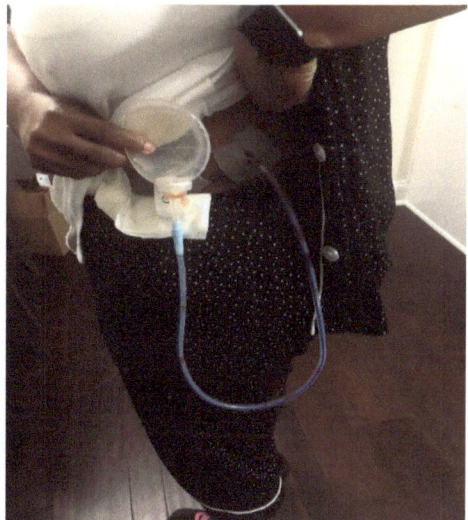

Reconstruction still in effect! This is a picture of one of the two drains tubes that I had after my 3rd surgery. Having these tubes were horrible!

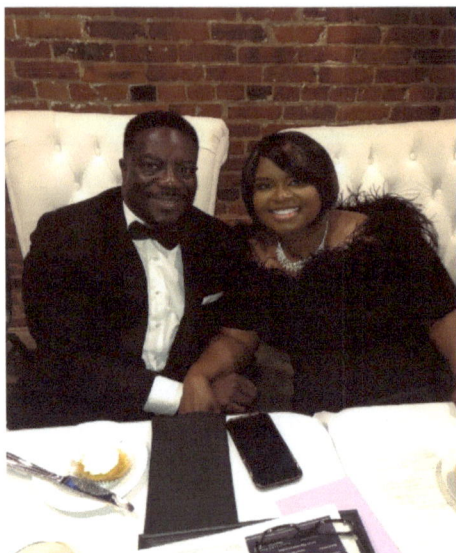

My knight in shining armor, my sweetheart, my Hershey kiss, my rock, my husband, Deshawn.

Pastor Gala 2019.

Gala 2019 loading! My beautiful family...I couldn't have walked this journey without them. I have nothing but love for these people. ❤️

Our town's very first cancer walk that my church and I sponsored. I'm wearing the shirt that I designed especially for the walk.

Church photo opt with one of my besties, Chelice Waites. She's such a sweetheart!

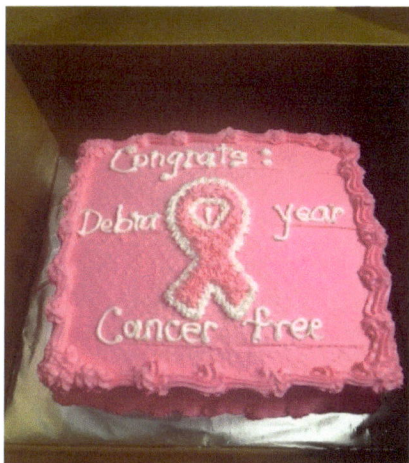

My sister surprised me with this cake, celebrating my 1st year being cancer free! It was my favorite, key lime!

Today I received my certificate and rang the bell for the second time since I finished chemo and all my infusions.

The Unexpected Game Plan
What Kind Of Prognosis Is This?

Today is May 23rd, and I have an appointment with the breast surgeon. I am not looking forward to this, but I knew I needed a game plan and he was chosen for the task of giving me one. I already had questions ready for him, hoping that he would answer the way I wanted him to. But that did not happen at all! I was about to meet a man that was going to change my life forever; there's no turning back from this!

My doctor's office was located in downtown Charleston, South Carolina. Charleston is a very historic and beautiful city. One thing I love about Charleston is that it's called the "Holy City" because of all the church steeples. It makes me feel as if God is there.

On the way to my appointment, my husband and I were listening to the radio in the car. This particular station is always playing motivational uplifting music, but today was a total shocker! A sad song came across the airwaves talking about someone having cancer. We have never, I mean never heard this song play on this radio station and we listen to this all the time!! My husband was taken back to the song and shocked. I was shocked and truly in disbelief of what I was hearing! After hearing a few lyrics of this cancer song, I reached out quickly and turned the station. What a way to start the day off right! That was not uplifting at all, not by a long shot!

We made it to the doctor's office safely. I said safely because the traffic in Charleston is horrible! It is a sea of cars going in every direction! Everybody was trying to get somewhere including us. With that being said, we made it to the office safely. Once I checked in, of course paperwork had to be filled out and an exchange of insurance cards and identification cards; you know the preliminary stuff that goes on. Filling out family history can be depressing because it seems as if I was checking off everything that the paper was asking. I have a family history of heart disease, diabetes, and even cancer. You name it, it is in the family. I wish I could put in *LOL* beside that but I cannot.

The nurse was ready for me and so I went. My husband and I entered the small room, and of course I got undressed from the waist up. The doctor walked in and introduced himself, shook our hands and proceeded to talk. I looked at this man for a long time because he looked so young. I was wondering if he really knew what he was doing. He did an exam on my breasts, and had a little small talk while he was doing that. His disposition was kind and concerning. He left the room, and I got dressed and he came back with a game plan.

When I tell you, everything that I prayed to God about was dismissed by this doctor, believe it was! My whole world was shattered into pieces like a broken mirror. I just knew that God heard my prayers about the situation, and that everything will work out just as I had petitioned God. By the words of this doctor, it truly did not seem like He did. Everything I prayed against; I was now being told that I will have to go through. I prayed to God to not have a mastectomy, and to not have to undergo chemotherapy. I did not want to lose my breast or hair. I was already struggling with alopecia and because of that I was losing my hair. I thought to myself, *"Now this!"*

Dr. K started his dissertation about my prognosis. He explained that my cancer was driven by the HER2 positive proteins, which makes the cancer more aggressive. When I heard that, I wanted to throw my hands up and just leave. I had not heard anything worthwhile or positive yet! I felt crushed! To hear that you have cancer is a blow by itself, but now to hear that you have a protein that is attached to the cancer cells that are making this cancer more aggressive is even worse. I just wanted to hear some good news; that's all! Because of the invasive and non-invasive cancer cells in my breast, Dr. K suggested chemotherapy to me. He wanted to see if the cancerous tumor would shrink. If the tumor did not shrink after aggressive chemo treatments, then I would have to have surgery. What kind of prognosis is this? I surely was not expecting this slap in the face! He told me that he was going to send me to Dr. S, an oncologist, and she will prescribe aggressive chemo treatment.

Everything was out of my hands! I had no control in this matter! This diagnosis and prognosis are happening to me, my body, and I have no say about it. I mean I can say, *"I refuse all treatments;"* however, then I would have this disease rapidly mutating inside of me. I understood that I did not have a choice in this matter. Knowing that this situation was totally out of my hands was the scary part! I knew how to trust God working through the doctors. I petitioned God for divine healing without surgery or treatments. While I wanted it to be done my way, I realize that God's ways are not my ways. His thoughts are not my thoughts.

The ride back home was quiet. I just looked out of the window while tears were streaming down my face. I was not up for having a discussion about what took place. I just wanted to go home, get under my covers and not come out. I was still hoping and praying that this was a horrible dream that I was experiencing. As soon as we got home, I headed straight for my room and got in bed. Being diagnosed with cancer does have an emotional affect on you. I did not feel like being bothered with anyone or anything. I just wanted to be left alone.

Needless to say, that did not happen. Minutes later, my husband came into the room and told me that the mayor called him to come to the town's meeting for something. I think it was to do the prayer. Sarcastically in my mind, I was saying, *"Okay. What does that have to do with me? Can't you see me laying in this bed?"* Of course, I said, *"Okay"* when he asked me to go with him. If anyone knows me, I enjoy supporting others, especially my husband. He is a well-known pastor and prominent figure in our town, and he is respected by many. I got up with my scrubs still on from work earlier that morning. He looked at me and asked me to change into something a little casual. Now I have to reluctantly find something nice to wear while trying my best to put on a happy face!

Once the meeting started, I noticed they had someone else praying, so I thought they might have had my husband on the agenda for something else. As time progressed, the meeting was near to a close and I heard the mayor talking about a familiar story. He was telling the story of me saving a baby's life Thanksgiving 2018. I am looking in bewilderment because that had nothing to do with my husband. Then the mayor called me up. Now I get it, my husband tricked me to come to this meeting. The mayor presented the *Silver Crescent Award* that the governor of South Carolina awarded to me. This is the highest award that a civilian can get in the state of South Carolina! I was blown away! All I could do was smile and thank the mayor. If only he knew the drastic, heartbreaking news that I had just received a few hours ago, he would have actually wondered, *"Why am I at this meeting?"* I spoke a little about the incident, and thanked the mayor, council members and governor for this remarkable award. Before going back to my seat, we had to take pictures. Of course, I called my husband up to the front with me to take a few pictures. After all was said and done, the meeting was adjourned and we came back home. Once we got home, my husband told me that he was hoping the award would make me happy after what just took place at the doctor's office. It did for a little while. I was very thankful and humbled by the award. Like I always said, I did it because that baby was in distress, and I did not do it for recognition.

Trying to keep normalcy in our lives, we were looking forward to JoyFest at Carowinds on Saturday in North Carolina. There were going to be people from all walks of life having a great time listening to some very talented gospel artists. Our youth group from the church was going and they were excited. Once inside the park, the kids and adults began riding the amusement park rides, and I was enjoying seeing them have fun. Hearing the music and the crowd, we knew that the concert had begun. Our group made our way to the amphitheater where the concert was taking place. We heard songs from Johnathan McReynolds and Travis Greene. I love these guys' songs; I listen to them all of the time.

After the concert, I could not leave without getting some turkey legs for my boys and I. Oh, how delicious they were! We stopped to get a bite to eat, then we headed home. It was hard *"acting"* normal while I felt miserable inside. I had to smile and laugh and enjoy myself knowing I had this disease growing in my body. Funny, how life throws you a curveball when you least expect it. Thanksgiving 2018, I was saving the life of a seven-month-old baby and in May of 2019, I was fighting for my life.

Perspectives In The Storm
Test, Test, Test

On Friday, May 31, 2019, I was scheduled to have a lymph node biopsy under the right arm. I traveled back to Mt. Pleasant through horrendous traffic, but I made it. Dr. K scheduled this procedure to see if the cancer had spread to my lymph nodes. The crazy part about this ordeal is that the lump I found was not the cancerous tumor. The discharge was not from the cancer either. The discharge and lump were a papilloma in my milk duct in my breast. The cancerous tumor was found closer to my chest wall in the right breast. Because of the location of the tumor, Dr. K ordered this biopsy to rule out the lymph nodes. I was bracing myself for the pain I had to endure, but it really was not as bad as I expected. Although it was very much unpleasant, the pain was not nearly as bad as the breast's biopsy.

I checked in to the Women's Center and waited patiently for my turn. The tech, Ms. B took me back and we went into an exam room. I changed into a gown and got on a bed. Ms. B began the first part of the procedure by locating the lymph nodes with a sonogram. She took pictures of the placement of the nodes so the doctor would know which one seems good to biopsy. Dr. H came into the room; she was the doctor that performed my breasts biopsies. She introduced herself again and got straight to work. She and Ms. B were discussing the pictures and decided on which ones to do.

She gave me the topical numbing agent to numb the area and then made a little slit into my skin. I was trying to pay attention to what she was doing and trying to keep my composure. I was somewhat fascinated by the procedure but I didn't like it because it was happening to me. She used some kind of probe to collect the cells as a specimen for the test. She went to two locations of lymph nodes and biopsied them. Then she went back and placed metal clips where she biopsied and she was through. I was sitting there thinking, *"I have never had my body violated like this before."* I was tired of being poked, prodded and we were just getting started.

Life was still going on around me. Two prominent women from our community passed away. These women were icons in our small town, and they will truly be missed. On Sunday my sister, another young lady and I went to eat some seafood. The food was divine, especially the crab legs, my favorite. Although my sister knew what was going on with me, it was hard trying to keep it together. I still committed to not telling anyone about my cancer diagnosis and she was not either. In the following coming weeks, I knew I was going to have doctor appointments so I decided to tell my CFO, office manager, and the head nurse at my job. I told them individually but I should have opted to tell them collectively. It made me sad and depressed just to hear myself mention the word cancer. Of course, I got hugs from them and empathy but I also got encouragement. My CFO told me that I can have a five-minute pity party, and then I had to move on and face it. There were times that I had to take my five-minute pity parties. Afterwards I wiped my tears, cleaned myself up and I moved on, so they say.

On Wednesday, June 5th, I had my initial appointment with the oncologist, Dr. S. Of course, I dreaded disappointment. This woman is about to tell me about toxins going into my body to kill this awful disease and it's going to make my little bit of hair fall out completely. Ugh! *This is unfair! I ask God, "Why is this happening to me? Why is this not happening to a conceited woman, or women who only thought of themselves, women who look down on other people. Why me?"* I actually asked the Almighty this! I just could not figure out why He kept allowing the enemy to beat up on me like this! What did I do to deserve this punishment!!

We checked into Charleston Oncology. As I internalized these moments, I felt as if I signed my life away with those documents I completed. The nurse took my husband and I to a room, and we waited to see the doctor. Dr. S walked into the room with a friendly smile on her face. She did not look to have much makeup on; she was just a natural pretty young face. She introduced herself and shook our hands. She asked me questions about the discovery of the lump and about how I was doing. Then she got right down to business. She did a physical exam and began to explain the plan for me. She was giving me a drug cocktail consisting of four different drugs by the name of CCHP. CCHP chemo stands for Taxotere, Carboplatin, Herceptin and Perjeta. The regimen was through a mediport, every three weeks for six months. Dr. S continued to explain to me that my cancer was driven by the HER2 protein. I had an over expression of the HER2 protein on my breast cells which caused my cancer to be HER2 positive.

All this information became overwhelming! Before starting chemo, she set me up to have a CT scan and a bone scan along with getting a mediport put in for chemotherapy. I had my work cut out for me while this disease was growing in my body, my breast. Dr. S scheduled my appointments very quickly. On June 7th, I pretty much spent the afternoon in West Ashley. The waiting room was covered with sick people and I was one of them. The waiting room was almost filled to capacity with people waiting on chemo treatments, scans and regular doctor visits. I was overwhelmed again! I just sat looking around at all these people. My husband and our two youngest boys were with me.

I picked up a magazine and began reading. Of course, it was a magazine about cancer, so I could not get away from the C word even if I wanted to. I was sitting there waiting for my scan, so I began to read an article about cancer and how it affected a woman's marriage. *REALLY?* This is not what I needed to be reading; however, it peaked my interest. While reading, a young tech came and asked me, *"Is everything alright?"* His name was Billy. I will never forget the special kind soul that was sent to me on that day. Billy handed me this bottle to drink before my scan. Needless to say, this drink was not appetizing at all. *Ugh, the horror but I had to finish it all!* I felt like the green vomit emoji. While the drink was doing its work, I continued reading. The article was interesting and sad. Because this woman was having a mastectomy, she developed emotional and physical distress which caused her marriage to fall apart. Although reading this could have discouraged me, it didn't. Because like the lady in the article, I too, was battling in my mind if my husband would leave me because I have to get a mastectomy. I wondered, *"How would he look at me? Would I be viewed as a whole woman still or a half of woman? Would he still want to be intimate with me and I with him?"*

Billy came to get me for my CT scan. Like I said before, he was a very kind soul and very caring. He started by explaining to me about the scan and the test. Then he warned me that what I drank will make me feel like I am using the bathroom on myself while going through this scan. Well, thanks Billy for the heads up because the drink did just that! I thought I literally was peeing on myself. It was a very uncomfortable feeling but I got through it. Once the test was over, Billy asked me when I was diagnosed. I told him; then he started encouraging me. He saw the tears and engulfed me in his arms, and we cried together. God knew what I needed at that moment and He sent me Billy. He did not rush me from the back, he just let me cry. I needed that release. I thanked Billy, and was off to my next appointment later on that afternoon.

The family and I went for a bite to eat before my next appointment. It was good to get away from it all; even if it were only for a little while. I was thankful that my husband and sons came with me that day. They have been a great support! My next appointment was a bone scan. To my surprise, that sweet little tech who was doing my scan was Billy's wife! Knowing that, made me smile; I knew I was in caring hands. I didn't like this test. I don't suffer from claustrophobia, but this scan was really discomforting. I felt like my face was a little too close to the top of this machine. My breath got short and I felt like I was about to panic. This has never happened to me! I had to find something to focus on fast. I started looking at this light. I kept my eyes fixed on that light and tried to bring my breathing back to normal. I felt a little relieved when I heard Billy's wife's voice saying *"It was almost over."* Thank you, Jesus! Thank you, Jesus! Once finished, I was too happy to jump off that machine, no help needed. It was truly a testing day, and I was ready to go home.

Having a cancer diagnosis seems to put things on hold in your life. While life is happening all around you, you feel like you are in this bubble of this fog. All alone, I felt like I was in a dream this whole time, praying that someone would wake me from this horror. During the midst of this horror, my baby sister had a birthday. She turned twenty-nine, and I was thrilled at how God was blessing her life! She was one of my constants in this situation. I needed a big sister and she was just that.

My family and I took my husband out to Red Lobster to celebrate Father's Day. I always enjoy celebrating others, especially my husband. I could not ask for a better man to be a role model for our sons. Not only is he a father to our three sons, but also, he is a spiritual father to others. He is a great pastor to the flock that God has given to him. He deserves to be celebrated.

Throughout this ordeal, my breast surgeon would call to keep me informed of the results and tumor board meetings. All doctors that dealt with cancer patients would come together to discuss the cases. I was one of the lucky ones (*being very sarcastic*) that they discussed a couple of times. After one of the meetings, Dr. K called me at work. I always left room for good news but somehow that good news did not find me. I heard Dr. K tell me the most devastating words that I did not want to hear. He and the tumor board looked at my scans and tests and determined that I needed to have a mastectomy! You talk about a sucker punch to the stomach. My breath was taken away! More tears, more anger, and more hurt. When can I get some good news? When will this evil ever end? He scheduled another MRI breast biopsy because the left breast had appeared to have similar traits as the breast on the right. I could not believe what I was hearing. I fell to pieces and the dam broke again. Once more, I could not help but cry!

My breast biopsy was on June 17, 2019 at 12:45 PM. I dreaded this whole ordeal. Once again, I am going to have an MRI, and get my breasts drilled into. I think this time, some tears came while the doctors were performing the procedure. I had two doctors this time working on me at the same time. I wondered to myself, *"Geesh! Can a sister get a break?"* It was so painful; all the pain, all the pain! I saw Dr. K on June 20th for the results. Thankfully, what the tumor board thought they saw was not on the MRI for the left breast. Oh, how I was relieved but it confirmed that I needed a mastectomy on the right breast. I could not imagine losing both breasts let alone one! I did not want to lose any at all! God, please help me, please!

Losing A Part Of Me
Half Or Whole

No one ever wants to experience losing a limb or a body part; no one wants to even think that way. I could not imagine in 1 million years that this was about to happen to me. Me! I was really trying to wrap my head around the fact of actually losing my breast! I am losing a part of me, a part of my body, a part of what makes me a woman! I would never be the same again, never! Dr. K referred me to Dr. M, a plastic surgeon who does natural replacement of breast implants. I had the option of using my own body to re-create a breast or using an implant; I chose the natural side. I saw Dr. M on June 27th at noon for the first time. Her office was very quiet, pleasant and calming. The office was decorated in soft pinks, yellow and aqua colors along with mermaids. I saw that she liked mermaids! The patients' rooms were cozy as well. She had pink gowns for her patients. I was really impressed. Even though I was there because I was losing my breast, the atmosphere was somewhat soothing.

Dr. M walked in my room and introduced herself. She wore quirky colored glasses and her hair was pulled back into a ponytail. She was very nice and caring. I asked her how she was and when I was having my surgery. We discussed that for a little while and then she explained to me the process of natural breast implant surgery. She examined me and took photos. She kept asking me if I was *okay*. She said most people tend to cry once they get to her office and was wondering if I was okay. My husband was with me and she even asked him if I was feeling fine. He told her yes. She was just amazed at how I was holding up. I was amazed at myself and I did not break down and sob like a baby. I went through the session with her without any tears. Before leaving, she set an appointment for me to go to the Imaging Specialist of Charleston for a scan. Another test, wonderful!

My appointment for the scan went well. It was like the other scans I had within the last couple of months. Just adding it to the list, literally. July 2019 ,3 has arrived. I had to be at the hospital by 7:00 AM to get prepped for surgery. I am getting prepped for Dr. K to remove my breast, my cancerous breast. Ugh, I hate cancer with a passion, I mean a serious passion! But at this point I can't change anything, no turning back now. I saw Dr. K before surgery, we talked for a little while. The surgical nurse and anesthesiologist came in and I talked with them as well. I told the anesthesiologist to make sure I am not aware of what is about to take place. I did not want to feel the pain or even wake up during the surgery. He told me he would give me a good cocktail and just smiled.

My husband told me the surgery took about six hours. I awakened to a room full of immediate family. Although it was great seeing them, I was kind of looking at them through squinted eyes. The cocktail that I received was very strong. I could barely keep my eyes open and my speech was not altogether. My sister said I was feeling good! My family was laughing at me. I remember her asking me if I wanted a kiss and I told her no because she does not kiss people. They all thought that I was hilarious! My husband told me the surgery lasted longer than the surgeon expected due to the fact that he wanted to get everything; he did not want to leave anything behind. I was fortunate enough to keep my nipples and areola. My doctor was able to save them. The cancer was closer to my chest wall and there were no signs of cancer close to the nipple.

When I looked down, it looked like one side of my chest collapsed. I was really asymmetrical, lopsided, and just uneven. My chest looked like a deflated misshaped balloon. I was devastated! To add insult to injury, I had this tube with a bulb attached underneath my arm. This was a tube used to drain the excess blood from the incision. My incision went from one side of my breast to the other. Well, what's left of it. So many different emotions flowing through me like different streams flowing into an ocean. *Hurt. Anger. Pain. Grief. Letdown. Furious. Helplessness.*

I questioned myself, *"How could a loving God allow His daughter to go through such a traumatic event? Doesn't God know that this could very well change her views of Him? Didn't God know that this would change the way she viewed herself now? God must know because He is the all-knowing God, the omniscient God, the one she believes in."* These questions played over and over in my mind like a broken record. I did not have any answers to them. My emotions stood as fortified statues, signifying their strengths against my logic and beliefs. They were yelling, screaming at God for not rescuing me from this torture. While on the other hand, my logic and beliefs were quietly whispering to me, *"The cancer is gone and you are still here. Bless God."* The scripture Romans 8:28 states "For God works all things together for good to those who love Him and are called according to his purpose." 2 Corinthians 12:9 states, "And He said unto me, My grace is sufficient for thee: for my strength is made perfect in weakness. Most gladly therefore will I rather glory in my infirmities, that the power of Christ may rest upon me," These scriptures began to whisper in my ear as well.

I felt like I was in a tug of war in my mind. It felt like I was on an amusement ride of highs and lows and I just wanted it to stop! I wanted to get off this emotional roller coaster, but I could not. This was my ride, my story and I did not have the power to change anything, stop anything or even erase any events. All I had the power to do was embrace, accept, and move forward. Even that was hard for me to do! I was on the other side of receiving the advice that I would normally tell one of my parishioners. This was a hard pill to swallow.

July 4th came and it was not all fireworks, fun, and hot dogs on a grill for me. I was being released from the hospital. I was going home feeling like half of a woman, feeling inadequate. The notion of not having my breast was turning over and over in my mind. The sadness creeps in over me like a dark and evil shadow. I did everything to hold back my tears, the dam that I felt was about to break in my soul. This was one of the longest rides home ever. Nature seemed extra quiet that day, no stirring while we drove down highway 41.

Finally, I was home, and all I wanted to do was go lay in my bed. I did not feel like being around anyone but I was glad to see my sons. Being in the presence of my family always warms my heart even in a trying time like this. I spoke to my boys and headed straight to my bedroom. I needed to just be by myself as I needed some space and time to process this part of the trial. Looking down at my chest was extremely hard. The familiar question started to arise in my mind and I fought to keep them from overtaking me. I just laid there in the bed in my own world.

The days ahead were not all that great. I was thankful to be alive, I really was but this ordeal was getting the best of me! I was thankful that the cancer was out of my body but also weary because the cancer took my breast along with it. Finding the courage to look at myself in the mirror was daunting. My new form of life was heartbreaking. The tears came streaming down my face because a part of me was now gone. The nurse navigator told me I would grieve like I literally lost a loved one and I did just that. Sometimes, I still experience grief quietly. Underneath my arm was sore due to my doctor removing my lymph node that was close to the side of the cancer. I felt really crummy but I did not show it. I kept it to myself. I did not want to worry my boys nor my husband. I tried to live a normal life and it was extremely hard, extremely hard!! I had to keep rehearsing 2 Corinthians 12:9 when God told Paul that His Grace was sufficient. This scripture spoke to me day in and day out; it spoke to me while my face was drowning with tears as I muffled the cries of my heart. That scripture was my safety net, my warm blanket, and my consolation when the pain was unbearable emotionally and mentally.

On Thursday, July 11th, was my post-op appointment with Dr. K. He checked the suture and removed the drain tube. That drain tube was horrible! He told me and my husband that he will be in surgery with me on Friday morning as well. He was going back into my chest and taking out more tissue to make sure my margins were clear. He would do that then Dr. M will put in the tissue expander. Two surgeries in one! Geesh! More going under anesthesia, here we go again. I did not have to be at the hospital too early this time because my surgery was at 1:30 PM. After checking in and getting prepped for surgery, the nurse had to put this inflatable warming blanket on me. It felt really good but weird as well. I have never seen anything like it before. Dr. M came into my room and spoke to me and my family before the surgery. We said a word of prayer then they took me into the operating room. The surgery lasted approximately four to five hours.

My anesthesia cocktail was not too bad! I woke up to see my family again which was always a pretty sight. My mom stayed with me this time at the hospital because my husband had a house blessing to do. He was going to stay but I insisted that he go. This would give him a break from all of this cancer craziness that we were experiencing.

My mom was great company! She had me laughing practically all night. Between her crazy mishaps and the nurse checking on me every two to three hours, I did not get much sleep at all. Morning came very quickly. I was hoping that I would get to go home, and I did. It does not seem possible to get adequate rest in the hospital. The doctor came in and we spoke for a while.

My husband and son came to the hospital and I was glad to see them. He was my ride home and I missed him too. My doctor said everything looked good; she gave me the rundown on what to do and what not to do. Then she said that I could go home; I was waiting on that. My husband and son left to pull up the car. Then my doctor shared some intimate things about a situation in her life. I was wondering, *"Why is she sharing this with me?"* I began to minister and encourage her because that is all I know to do. At that moment, my situation did not matter. It did not matter that I was lying in a hospital bed. It did not matter that I had a foreign object in my chest. It did not matter that I was the patient. It just did not matter! What mattered was that I was on an assignment, and quite frankly, I did not know that I was until later on during my journey.

Chemo
Do I Have To Go?

On August 12th, I began my journey with Dr. S. She had my new chemo regimen set for me. Dr. S shared with me and my husband the details of this regimen. She scheduled my echocardiogram and my mediport procedure. She explained that the medicine they will administer to me affects the heart. Initially, I was afraid to take this type of medication because there is a history of heart disease in my family. All I could do was think about my dad who passed away from myocardial infarction, a heart attack. Now I felt like I had something else to worry or be concerned about along with the side effects from chemo. This was just too much on my plate!! I was already tired prior to beginning chemo.

To make life seem simple and blissful my wonderful husband planned a family vacation to Kentucky! I was ecstatic and so were the kids. We tried to keep the normalcy in our lives while this chaos was going on, and he did a much better job of it to tell you the truth. He stayed positive even through my not so positive days. I do not think I could ever repay him for that. Our road trip to Kentucky was a blast! We stopped in Tennessee, and hopped on a helicopter to view the city. That was incredible and we all enjoyed it! Once we left there, we grabbed some lunch and we made our trip to Kentucky. Now, we were very excited to go but it was a long trip! We were all happy when we got to the hotel to really stretch out.

The next morning, we were off to the Ark Encounter in Williamstown, Kentucky. This was massive! It was built to the same coordinates of the ark that was built in the Bible by Noah. I could not believe my eyes. We were excited and ready to take the tour. I advise everyone to go visit this beautiful piece of work. You will be fascinated! We walked through and up the levels with amazement at the different animals and how they were portrayed. The experience was mind blowing and seeing all of this actually made me think out of the box about the Bible story of Noah, his family, and the ark.

After viewing the ark for about three to four hours, we went to the small zoo that was there. The animals were cool to see as well. We were there just taking in the rest of the sites like the shops, restaurants and theater. It was a fun filled and impactful day. We all thoroughly enjoyed it. While on this vacation, I had to take pictures of my incision to send to Dr. M, so she can keep up with my progress. That was very strange to do, but I did it! The incision was healing well with no problems.

August 15th was day two of our vacation. We drove to Cincinnati, Ohio and toured the city. We drove over the bridge that connected Kentucky and Ohio, and that was cool too. We also went to the aquarium and we had so much fun. I took pictures of Kenly and Jordan with their heads in an alligator's mouth! Of course, they made it exciting and scary with their facial expressions. I smiled and thought to myself, *"my men."* On the next day, my husband surprised me, and the boys by taking us to Indianapolis, Indiana. We toured the city and went to dinner. I was like a little kid in a candy store! The city was pretty busy. We went by the Lucas Oil Stadium a couple of times to take pictures. Then we headed to the Cheesecake Factory. I was in love! The food was delicious from the bread to the entrée to the cheesecake! The cheesecake... *"MMM."* Everything was just perfect, and I enjoyed every bit of it!

I was kind of sad a little because I knew we were leaving Saturday morning to come back to reality. Reality for me was doctor appointments and my procedure for my mediport. These things were ugly constant reminders of me having cancer and cancer taking my breast. I remained positive and happy around the family because I did not want them to know I was feeling that way. We started our long trek back home to South Carolina. I had a great time with my men as I like to call them. We really enjoyed this time together; we laughed, relaxed, ate good food, and laughed even more. This trip was well needed and will always be one of my favorites!

The week of August 19th through the 24th was filled with appointments. From seeing my plastic surgeon, to getting an echocardiogram, to the inserting of my mediport for chemo, and finally chemotherapy education on Thursday. I am telling you, Mount Pleasant and Charleston South Carolina have become my home away from home since this disease invaded my life. I could not believe, did not want to believe that in a few days, I was going to be injected with toxic chemicals to kill off any cancer cells that may be left in my body. I had to have twelve rounds of chemo and steroids. Geesh! Me and steroids do not get along!

September 3, 2019, was the first day of my chemotherapy treatments. The room was so cold and there were recliner stations all over. I was shocked at the number of stations and people. I found myself a little station away from most of the people. The station had a reclining chair, another regular chair for anyone who comes along and a small TV. I saw two other men in my area already hooked up to their machines. One was sleeping away and the other wide awake with his machine beeping loudly. I wondered to myself, *"How could you sleep with that noise?"*

My nurse came over to me and asked a few questions and started my toxic cocktail. She sprayed some cold topical anesthesia onto the port area and told me to take a deep breath. She then popped this needle-like device into the port. I was not ready to get started. The first part of my cocktail was fluids, Benadryl, steroids and an anti-acid medication. After that part was over another nurse came and started the Herceptin cocktail. This medicine was to target the HER2 neu protein receptors. After finishing that bag of meds which was about one to two hours long, the nurse came back with my chemotherapy, the poison. I was not too happy with this because all I could think about was there's about to be poison running through my veins and my body.

They allowed Deshawn, Kenly, and Jordan to come back to sit with me. I clearly remember looking at my husband and saying these words, *"This is depressing."* I did not want to be there at all, especially around other people who were going through the same thing. It was just too sad and heartbreaking but it was real. I was ready to go home. The nurse came back over to me with four ice packs, very cold ice packs. She told me that she was going to wrap my feet and I was to place my hands on the other two ice packs. This little trick is supposed to help with neuropathy that can happen in your extremities with chemo. Now this was ridiculous! Who wants to have ice packs on your hands and feet an hour or more? This was crazy to me! I mean am I not suffering enough?

The next few days after chemotherapy, I felt like I was not really prepared for the side effects at all. My doctor clearly left out pertinent information that could have at least given me a heads up. Experiencing nausea, severe indigestion, some constipation and just feeling awful! I would not wish this on my very worst enemy. I was scheduled for twelve rounds of chemotherapy. For twelve weeks, I had to experience this poison flowing through my veins killing off cancer cells that may have been in my body. Not only did chemotherapy kill cancer cells, but also it killed my fast-growing cells. With that being said, my hair began to fall out, my fingernails and toenails turned black and they ached extremely bad. I told my husband, *"I wish I could get my hands on a tool to pull my finger nails off!"*

By my second treatment, food was unpleasant! Foods that I love like butter pecan ice cream, tasted so sweet like I was eating a spoonful of sugar. Yuck! Some foods tasted extremely salty. By my third treatment, my sleep pattern was off, and I developed diarrhea. Oh, what joy! But what brought tears to my eyes was the start of losing my hair. I was already losing it due to alopecia slowly but now I am about to lose it all. I tell you, being diagnosed with cancer will affect your whole life. On day number six, I got a surprise! My friend, Lady Camesha Parrot came to take me to my chemo treatment. I was totally blown away! This lady drove two hours from Columbia, South Carolina to Andrews, South Carolina just for me. Then we had to drive another hour to Mount Pleasant for my appointment. What a sweet gesture she did for me! She was able to sit in the back with me and that was comforting. She got a chance to see exactly what I went through.

My side effects from the chemo got worse and worse. My whole body was itching like crazy after showering. I had bad indigestion, and my feet had a tingling sensation with each step I took. My face even started breaking out really bad. I had to go to my dermatologist because it was getting worse. My skin color changed; I got darker. Now that was something I was not expecting! That was a shocker for me!

Throughout the journey of my treatments, life still went on. My husband celebrated his 47th birthday by going out of town. Our oldest son took him out for the weekend. He needed to get away from the house and my dilemma! I was very glad, and supportive of this because he had been by my side since everything started and he needed a break.

My breast surgeon mentioned to me about having radiation therapy. I totally was against getting radiation. I really did not want to get it, if I didn't have to. I heard about the horrors of radiation and how it would prolong me from getting reconstruction surgery. I sought out a second opinion. I met with Dr. T from The Medical University of South Carolina. I was able to get in really quickly to see her. I knew that it was God on my behalf. At that appointment, she examined me thoroughly and made me very comfortable around her. She looked at my medical records and surgeries and said that my margins were clear so I did not have to have radiation. I could have shouted and danced all around that room! At that point, I felt like things were finally changing for me!

Sunday in church, my whole perspective changed about my cancer journey. My husband gave me a word from the Lord. He said that I had to go through this cancer ordeal because I had to meet a certain person. I had to minister to this person because they were going to kill themselves. He said that God was using me to minister to them to save their life. That hit me like a ton of bricks because I was only thinking of myself and how I felt. That day I changed my perspective.

On November 7, 2019, I woke up to some of the worst news ever. My best friend, Prophetess LaNola Goings passed away. This really broke my heart. She would always encourage me while I was going through my cancer journey. I am going to miss her terribly!

Hooray! November 19, 2019 will forever be sketched in my brain because this was my last day of chemotherapy. My family and some of my church members joined me as I took my last treatment. After I was through, I got to ring the bell! I was extremely excited because my treatments were finally over. We all walked over to the bell and I started my little speech like this, *"This is in honor of my Uncle James. He passed away in March from pancreatic cancer, my mother-in-law passed away seven years ago from pancreatic cancer and this is for my friend LaNola Goings. I lost her and I know she would have been here, so I am ringing this bell in honor of them."* I then proceeded to ring the bell. That was the most exhilarating feeling ever! The sound of that bell ringing never sounded so good.

We all were basking in the joy of me ringing the bell as we prepared to leave. All thirteen of us got on the elevator and then the unthinkable happened; the elevator stopped working between floors. No one panicked. We just called the operator and told them where we were. This was like a scene out of a movie! Firefighters came to put a ladder through the top opening of the elevator and we had to go through that small hatch! That was exciting too!

Once we were all out, of course while taking the stairs we laughed all the way down. The crew and I traveled to Longhorn's Restaurant for my celebration dinner. The celebration was great but I could not taste the food. Yay me! But just having family and friends there was all that mattered because I finished my chemotherapy, and they were there to see it and to see me through my journey. I was very grateful for them to witness this momentous victory!

Road To Construction: Physically & Spiritually Healing Is A Part Of God's Plan

Reconstruction surgery was in progress! The tissue expander was very tiring and heavy. I was ready for this device to get out of my chest. I continued my Herceptin infusions every three weeks for a year with Dr. S. Ugh! I was experiencing a Job moment because I was just waiting for my change to come. Waiting, waiting, and waiting. This process was tedious and exhausting. I truly lived out the attribute of long-suffering during this cancer journey.

Another Thanksgiving came, and this time the food tasted funny. I really could not pig out like I wanted to because my taste buds were not straight. Sweet potato soufflé, and the collards were not the best you know, but I got through it. I took my eyes off of the food and started thinking about how grateful I was for life. Holidays take on a new meaning now. Every day is more of a blessing now than ever. Holidays, celebrations, and life itself is truly a gift.

December arrived and that meant Christmas was finally here. While I was still experiencing chemo side effects that were very unpleasant, I manage to never stopped working throughout this experience. On this particular day, December 19, 2019, we had our tree trimming party. I had not taken any photos, but this day I did. I tried to get all the way in the back! My skin was extremely dark, and I gained weight in my face along with the rest of my body. I thought, *"OMG! I look horrible."* I could barely recognize myself! That felt awful, felt devastating emotionally. This was another hard blow, once again!

I fought the spirit of depression from the beginning of this journey. I was determined not to deal with this because I knew depression can be consuming. But I started feeling sad and lonely after the photo. My nurse navigator told me that I would have highs and lows but for some reason I was not expecting these feelings at this time! I broke my silence one day and told my husband how I was feeling. I don't think that was a good idea because I don't think he understood what was going on with me. I remember expressing to him that I felt like I was half of a woman. The mastectomy took more from me than I realized. His response was, *"I've never looked at you as half of a woman; I still love you.*" All of that was good, it was a great response but I wanted more. I needed more. I needed him to grab me and hold me. I needed him to just let me cry, sob, scream into his chest again, but nothing like that happened. I waited just to see if it was a delayed reaction to what I said but no movement. We had a few minutes of silence and I left the den and went into our bedroom. Feelings of sadness, frustration and discouragement were flowing through me, and all I could do was cry. While I wanted more, he could have only given me what he understood.

January 2020 arrived, and I was excited because all of our boys are turning a year older this month. Our middle son, Kenly is celebrating a milestone birthday. He is turning 16 years old. What are the odds that our god daughter's birthday is this month as well! Geez! Celebrations will literally be every week. Also, a very special day this month is our twentieth wedding anniversary. Twenty years is a long time to be with someone, but I would not have it any other way. My family means so much to me, and celebrations are even more special now more than ever before!

I started taking Tamoxifen on the sixth. I have to take this medication for five years. This medication was prescribed to reduce the risk of developing cancer again because I had DCIS. The only problem I have with this medication is that it causes hot flashes and night sweats. Oh, my goodness, these hot flashes are horrible! They happen at any time of the day or night. But it is something I have to deal with and there is no way around it.

I saw Dr. M on January 16, 2020 to discuss and set up a reconstruction surgery date. I was ready to get this over with. This has been a long tedious process. Dr. M and I settled on February 18th at 8:30 AM for my reconstruction surgery. *Woohoo!* Now I'm just counting down the days. While cancer never stops nor everything that goes along with it, I could not give up or quit the process. My God is going to take and make something great out of all of this!

Today is February 18th I had to be at Roper Hospital in Mount Pleasant at 6:30 AM. The time had finally arrived. This was very exciting because I was finally getting this tissue expander out of my chest! I was about to get a new breast! I was a little uneasy knowing that I would not be able to feel anything. Literally nothing. That would be an adjustment for me. While the nurse was prepping and poking me for surgery, Dr. M came to visit with me and my husband in the room. She asked me how I was doing and made sure I was ready. Before she left, we had a word of prayer, then it was time to rock 'n' roll. My husband kissed me, and they rolled me down the corridor to surgery.

After eight hours of surgery, I woke up in the ICU. There weren't any complications but Dr. M wanted me to have around the clock care. And it was definitely around the clock. I was checked on every two to three hours all day every day. There was an apparatus connected to my breast and all I could hear was the blood moving rapidly. This was the neatest thing because it was a great sign that the tissue took well. Dr. M surgically removed only half of the fat from my abdomen. She wanted to make sure that the tissue worked well with my body. After a few days of monitoring the tissue, we went back into surgery to remove the other part of my abdomen. I was in the hospital from February 18, 2020 to February 23, 2020. Following my release, I was scheduled to be out of work for six weeks for recovery.

During this time, churches, venues, restaurants, schools, and even jobs were shutting down due to the infectious virus called Coronavirus-Covid 19. We had to start wearing masks and gloves when we were out and about. We couldn't congregate at church because the virus was spreading so fast. Everything everywhere was in survival mode. While staying safe, I was still recovering and going to my Herceptin infusions every three weeks. This would be my last year taking them.

Post-op appointments went well. I was glad to get rid of the drain tubes. Like I said before, those things are the devil! It was awesome knowing that I was a donor to myself to form a new breast. God is truly amazing how He takes and transforms things. I have my new breast, and a flat stomach. Hallelujah! I am beginning to finally ease back into life as a woman, and not feel like I am half of one. Blessings to the most High God!

Epilogue

Since my initial surgery for my mastectomy on July 3, 2019, I have had a total of eleven surgeries. My final surgery was on June 18, 2021. It has been an exhausting journey, but God has not failed me yet. I want to encourage you to keep living, keep striving, keep fighting! Do not let the enemy blow out your flame. You are stronger than you realize, you can and will make it one day at a time. In Psalms 139:14 "God lets us know that we are fearfully and wonderfully made and that we are a part of HIS wondrous works". So we must not let this beautiful life go to waste. We are created to make an eternal impact in the earth and I believe you can do just that. Stay faithful to God, continue trusting Him because His grace is sufficient for you!